P9-ECV-269

CUT

This edition published in 2022

By SJG Publishing, HP22 6NF, UK

All rights reserved. No part of this work may be reproduced in any form or by any means, electronic or mechanical, including photocopying, recording or by any information storage and retrieval system, without the prior written permission of the publisher.

© Susanna Geoghegan Gift Publishing

Author: Rebecca Dickinson

Cover design: Milestone Creative

ISBN: 978-1-911517-95-5

Printed in China

10 9 8 7 6 5 4 3 2

CUT

How to lead a *simpler* life

CONTENTS

INTRODUCTION

crap

NOUN

1 Something of extremely poor quality.
2 Excrement.

VERB

1 Defecate.
2 Talk at length in a foolish or boring way.

Lexico.com

Do you ever feel like you are being fed a constant stream of unsolicited advice? Do you often feel caught between having too much, yet never enough? Are you fed up with being told what to eat, where to go, how to dress, what to buy, how to live and even what to think? Does the constant pressure to 'live your best life' leave you feeling physically and mentally exhausted? And who decides all this stuff anyway? Do you sometimes feel as if you have lost connection with what it is you really want from life, or the person you really want to be? If so, it's time to cut the crap and let go of junk, on both the inside and the outside.

Whether it's bodily waste, worthless objects or unwarranted opinion, crap is, by definition, stuff that we don't really need. From the tsunami of plastic to the mountains of processed food and mass-produced clothing, to the excess of electronic gadgets, flat-packed furniture and storage 'solutions' designed to contain all the other crap we don't actually need, the earth is in danger of becoming a shrine to crap.

But of course, crap is not just the physical stuff, it's also the messages that are drip-fed to us hour by hour, week by week, like mainline drugs until they become our own opinions – until we can no longer hear ourselves think. And it's the crap that we buy into that drives our actions, causing us to clog up our lives and the planet with more and more junk, like fatty deposits slowly suffocating the arteries of the world. Cutting the crap therefore starts with questioning social expectations and standing up to consumerist norms. It involves calling out the bullshit and repossessing our thoughts, because the way we think determines the way we live.

CHAPTER 1

CUTTING THE CRAP IN YOUR HEAD

Every waking hour of every day we are bombarded with messages, both directly and indirectly, that urge us to conform, to comply, to aspire, to desire, and ultimately to consume. Messages that promise life can be better, we can be happier, healthier, calmer, thinner. Messages that pretend to have our best interests at heart, when the real objective is to make us feel inadequate or lacking in some way. Messages that tell us we are not interesting, or attractive, or acceptable enough as we are. Why? So that we buy the product that will put everything right. Unfortunately, these messages can become the tune inside our heads, rather like an annoying 80s hit you can't unhear.

And when we buy into the crap we hear, we end up jumping on the crapwagon and filling our heads, bodies, homes and ultimately the planet, with junk, in the hope of discovering lasting bliss or instant success. But of course this rarely happens. This is because true fulfilment starts on the inside: with learning to be happy with who we are and what we have, rather than striving for more, or trying to be someone we are not.

'The privilege of a lifetime is
to become who you truly are.'
C.G. JUNG

Crap versus authenticity

Staying true to ourselves can be a tough call in an image-obsessed, acceptance-driven, 'fake it until you make it' culture. We live in a world where it's increasingly difficult to separate the crap from the truth, where little is as it seems. A world where food is only as good as it looks on Instagram, where bodies are airbrushed and a selfie can stand in for identity, where having a persona trumps being a real person, where politicians lie, fake news flourishes and brands pretend to be our friend. Perhaps the only certainty is that a huge amount of what we see and hear is based on crap – the very antithesis of authenticity.

What's more, it can be hard to be yourself in a world that's driven by a lack of authenticity. To be honest can leave us feeling vulnerable or exposed. As a result we try to adapt, to be accepted, to be relevant, to be somebody. We put on different masks for different occasions – the social media mask, the night-out mask, the professional mask, the great friend mask, even the relationship mask.

And in doing so we mask our real identities, not just from others, but eventually from ourselves as well. We spend so much time pretending to be someone or something we are not, that we become little more than an impersonator. But eventually the act becomes exhausting or something happens that causes the mask to slip, and like a fake piece of art we run the risk of being found out, or worse, of being deemed worthless. But there is an alternative: we can refuse to be swayed by the messages that become the crap inside our heads, and listen to ourselves instead. We can embrace authenticity – and this is where cutting the crap begins.

Keeping it real

When we succumb to the pressure to fit in, we hide our best asset: our own uniqueness. Being authentic simply means being yourself rather than a social cliché. It's about stripping away the fake exterior, avoiding all those tricks and filters and throwing off the mask. It's also about staying true to your values and beliefs, regardless of whether they go viral, or make you rich, or successful or popular. It's about being a real person, rather than an impersonation. Of course there are occasions where it's necessary to behave in a certain way – in a lecture, or at a funeral, or in a restaurant for example - but that doesn't mean we change our identity.

True authenticity takes guts: it can take strength to say what you mean or to express your real feelings, especially if it means going against the flow. But authentic people don't try to change their personality according to the situation; they remain genuine and grounded. However, just because you don't try to fit in with the masses doesn't mean you need to make a concerted effort to stand out.

Inevitably, businesses and social media have latched on to the demand for authenticity – only to turn it into yet another branding or bragging opportunity. But there is nothing authentic about claiming to be authentic simply to win customers, just as there as nothing authentic about contriving to be different. The meme 'be yourself' is often just a thinly veiled euphemism for 'show off'. True authenticity doesn't mean trying to prove yourself to the outside world; it's not a quest for recognition or attention or likes, it's about finding true meaning in our lives and living accordingly. What's more, being authentic isn't a goal, or something that can be ticked off like running a marathon or visiting Rome, it's an ongoing process of letting go of crap. And while it may not make you rich, or successful or popular, it will almost certainly make you happier than trying to be someone you're not.

> *'To be nobody but yourself in a world which is doing its best, night and day, to make you everybody else – means to fight the hardest battle which any human being can fight; and never stop fighting.'*
>
> E.E. CUMMINGS

How to be authentic

The road to authenticity can take courage, clarity and soul-searching. Crucially though, being authentic isn't something we do, it's something we are. It's about recognising how much of our lives are controlled by crap and staying away from or undoing all those things that make us inauthentic. It may be scary at first, but it's also enlightening and empowering, like the feeling you get when you fully connect with someone, or find something you truly love. Personal authenticity provides a deep sense of being at one with yourself which feels so much better than faking it. So here are six real ways to start cutting the crap and being yourself.

1. Stop caring about other people's perceptions

One of the root causes of inauthenticity is a desire to fit in. On the flip side, when we stop caring about other people's expectations, we become free to express our real feelings, beliefs and opinions. What's more, anyone who doesn't want to know the real you isn't worth knowing. So be proud of who you are and brave enough to stop worrying about how other people will judge you. In addition, when we are genuine, we encourage others to be genuine too. But if we hide behind masks, we encourage others to do the same and it's impossible to have fulfilling relationships with people if we only ever present a version of ourselves. It might help to grab a notebook and write down a list of thoughts about who you are and who you want to become, as well as the kind of person you don't want to be.

2. Embrace imperfection

We wear masks to hide our perceived shortcomings and flaws. Sometimes these masks are physical, in the form of make-up or even cosmetic surgery. Other times, they involve reining in or exaggerating our true emotions, pretending to be more or less than we really are. Being authentic involves accepting your flaws and allowing yourself to make mistakes in order to change and grow. Perfectionism, on the other hand, prevents us from truly accepting ourselves. Remember: none of us are the finished product.

3. Put down that bloody phone

If you couldn't go a day without a drink, you'd know you had a problem. Yet many of us can't go twenty minutes without our phones. No longer just a means of communication, phones have become a constant source of distraction, and in many cases, a full-blown addiction. We have become so dependent on them it's as if they are an inextricable extension of our forearms. We no longer control our phones, they control us. Yet it's impossible to experience life in an authentic way when you're constantly checking or scrolling, or comparing or curating your life for others to witness. And it's impossible to fully engage in a meal, a conversation or an experience, or to give someone your full attention, when you can't resist checking every buzz and ping. As well as being inauthentic, it's also rude, suggesting that a small yellow face is more important than the face in front you. So put the bloody thing down, or better still, put it out of reach. Giving someone your full attention, or fully immersing yourself in a situation, shows sincerity and intention and is one of the easiest ways to be more authentic.

4. Get back to nature

In the modern world, where reality can be so easily tempered with software, seeing is not necessarily believing. Yet sometimes, we just need to step outdoors to be reminded that there is still one unfaltering source of authenticity in the world. From the everyday miracle of sunrise, to the majestic mountains and tempestuous ocean, nature is perhaps the final fortress of reality; a rare source of truth, beauty and permanence in a fickle world. No filter required. It's well known that spending time in nature is great for health and well-being, helping to boost life satisfaction and lower the rate of conditions like anxiety and depression. But beyond that, there is a sense in which the powerful, unkempt authenticity of nature can inspire authenticity in our own lives too, stirring in us a desire to live in a way that reflects and supports the earth. On the other hand, the capacity of the human race to pollute and destroy highlights on a planetary scale the hideous consequences of living out of step with nature and filling the earth with crap.

5. Follow your passions – not the crowd

Can't get into yoga? Do something else. Game of Thrones not your thing? Watch something different. Prefer wellies to heels? Go for it! Being authentic involves exploring your interests and rocking your own style regardless of whether it's trending or not. It's so easy to focus on what other people are doing, and what other people have, and to feel like we need to emulate them in order to be accepted. (Although the irony is that they too are probably just following someone else.) So forget about what's going on in other people's lives and don't fall for the illusion that you need to be on-trend to be happy. Instead, focus on doing the things you genuinely love with the people you love.

6. Have fun!

Nothing is more authentic than pure, unadulterated fun. So immerse yourself in the moment rather than analysing it, or sharing it on social media. Enjoy the cake and forget how it looks on Instagram, swim in the sea without worrying about whether you have a 'beach body' (you have a body, that's all that matters) and laugh with your kids instead of posting all their achievements on Facebook. What's more, life is way more enjoyable when we stop taking ourselves so seriously and revel in the fun while it lasts.

'You will be what you must be, or else you will be nothing.'

JOSÉ DE SAN MARTÍN

Cutting negative thoughts

If we take the crap in our heads to be the stuff that we don't want, then for many of us that includes a large bunch of negative thoughts. These thoughts can arise when we think we need to look or act a certain way to be accepted, or when we compare ourselves to others.

But have you ever wondered how many thoughts you have per day? According to scientists, the answer is a rather mind-blowing 70,000. That's around 3,000 thoughts per hour. Unfortunately, quantity doesn't necessarily mean quality – around 95 per cent of these thoughts are said to be repetitive, while around 80 per cent of them are negative (which probably explains why there aren't more creative geniuses in the world). You could do the maths if you wanted to, but basically that's an awful lot of recycled mental crap festering in our already overloaded brains. Now imagine the possibilities if you were able to get rid of the rubbish and make headspace for the good stuff.

The trouble with mental crap is that it manifests itself in the rest of our lives too. Negative thoughts translate into the things we say and do and the way we feel. For example, if we constantly tell ourselves that we won't succeed at something – whether it's passing an exam, getting a promotion, finding love or beating anxiety – we probably won't. Instead, we just diminish the will to try, further increasing the probability of failure. This, of course only reinforces our existing mindset and gives that sneering inner voice another opportunity to say, 'I told you so!'

Put simply: negative thinking leads to negative behaviour, which leads to a negative outcome, which creates more negative thoughts, and so the cycle continues. Left unchallenged, we can end up trapped in a self-fulfilling and repeating pattern of failure and despair. Sadly, this can have a devastating effect on our mental health.

But there is an escape route. We don't have to accept the crap inside our own heads. We don't have to listen to the inner troll that bad-mouths and belittles us, that knocks us and mocks us, and prevents us from living the life we want; the life we deserve. Instead, we can change our internal dialogue and turn negative thoughts into positive ones. It may not be quite as easy as changing the channel on the TV, but it is possible. We just have to locate our inner remote control.

Breaking negative thought patterns

1. Recognise the signs

The first step towards defeating your inner critic is to be aware of when it opens its ugly mouth. Negative thoughts often include words such as 'never', 'should' and 'can't'. Set your inner radar to pounce on these words as soon as they appear, so that you can stop them before they make an impression. It can also help to work out when your inner critic is most active. For example, are you hardest on yourself when you have to speak in public, or talk to strangers or when you look in the mirror? Identifying when negative thoughts occur can help you to resist them and highlight areas of your life where you may need support.

Negative thoughts can also take the form of complaining or whingeing. Unfortunately, humans have a natural tendency to notice the bad stuff more than the good stuff thanks to something called the 'negativity bias'. This is believed to be a by-product of evolution, when having a 'nose for danger' would have helped our ancestors to stay safe, enabling them to focus on physical dangers such as savage wild beasts, rather than being distracted by something like a pretty flower.

In the modern world, physical threats are rare, but the ingrained negativity bias means that our minds overemphasise other sources of negativity instead. This explains why we are more likely to remember when someone puts us down rather than when they pay us a compliment, and why bad experiences affect us more strongly than good ones. So for example: you might feel a surge of anger or frustration when your train to work is delayed, but barely even register when it arrives on time.

2. Stop!

Recognising negative thoughts is great, but it's just the first step; now you need to take action. Imagine if you saw a lamb tangled up in a fence. Presumably, you wouldn't just stand there, you would go and set it free. It's the same with negative thinking. It's no use just standing still while destructive thoughts continue to hold you back – you need to let them go. You could simply yell 'stop!' and refuse to take any notice. Or you could reframe your negative thoughts in a positive light. So instead of looking in the mirror and telling yourself you hate your chunky thighs, remind yourself that these thighs get you out of bed every morning; they allow you to stand, walk, run, climb stairs and even mountains.

The same goes for complaining. Instead of focusing on the fact that your train is late, try to find something positive to say, such as: at least it wasn't cancelled, at least you have a job to go to which means you have an income, which means you can afford to buy food and do nice things. By making a conscious effort to change negative thoughts into positive ones, it's possible to train your brain to think differently. With time, positive thinking will become second nature leading to a boost in overall happiness.

We may not be able to control every situation, but we can control the way we think, and consequently the way we feel. As a result, this may actually lead to a change in outcome, because if negative thoughts tend to lead to negative results, imagine what could happen when you think positively.

3. Step away

In the same way as it's important to distance ourselves from toxic people, we shouldn't hang out with toxic thoughts either. Firstly, tell yourself it's not you speaking, it's your inner critic. You could even give this internal voice a stupid name to help diminish its power and separate it from the rest of your identity.

Secondly, remind yourself that your thoughts are merely thoughts. They are not real, they are not facts; they are just transient mental events that reflect your current mindset. This doesn't mean denying that a thought exists, it means recognising the difference between telling yourself: 'nobody finds me interesting' and telling yourself: 'I am having the thought that nobody finds me interesting.' In this way, you aren't endorsing the negative thought, you are simply acknowledging its existence, which is a subtle but important difference.

4. Take action

The ultimate way to silence negative thoughts is to get out there and prove them wrong. So if your inner voice tells you that you will never make new friends, or complete an assignment or learn to play the guitar, get out there and show it who's boss. Of course, when your self-esteem is on the floor, trying to get through even the tiniest task can feel like trying to take on the world. So start with small, achievable goals. It really doesn't matter how insignificant; every little accomplishment represents one less negative thought, and a step towards cutting the crap in your head.

'Watch your thoughts; they become words. Watch your words; they become actions. Watch your actions; they become habit. Watch your habits; they become character. Watch your character; it becomes your destiny.'

LAO TZU

CHAPTER 2

CUTTING THE CRAP ONLINE

With the explosion of the internet and social media, many of us are now online from the moment we wake up to the moment we slide our phones under the pillow. Young people in particular are more connected, yet more lonely and insecure than ever. Social media sites are no longer just a way of networking, but a tool for comparison, voyeurism and envy. And when we measure ourselves against others it's easy to feel like we don't measure up. Yet real happiness comes from living our own lives, rather than simply copying and pasting from the internet.

Through the impenetrable membrane of a screen, it can appear as if everyone else is having more fun, more success, more everything. This can lead to a cocktail of negative emotions: anxiety, jealousy, disappointment, discontentment, longing and of course the 21st century affliction of FOMO (the Fear Of Missing Out).

To assuage this fear, we end up trying to cram as much as possible into our lives – possessions, experiences, goals. But the constant choices and temptations are overwhelming, the conveyor belt is never-ending and we are never satisfied, adding to our stress and anxiety. Life becomes an inexhaustible list of must-dos and must-haves. And when this happens, we lose the ability to just be.

What's more, the buzz of ticking off an accomplishment or buying something new rarely lasts, and after a while our happiness levels return to their original setting. This explains why lottery winners are said to be no happier than non-winners eighteen months after cashing in their winning ticket. Psychologists refer to this as the hedonic treadmill, or hedonic adaptation. In other words: we very quickly adapt to nice things and once the novelty has worn off, it's easy to end up craving something else.

But there is one easy way to break free from this constant pressure and that is simply to reduce the amount of time you spend online. Because while the internet has become an essential part of the way we live and communicate, it's also become the primary source of mass-produced crap. From fake people to fake news, to be permanently logged in is to be swept along with the tide of crap. The result is that we end up believing things that aren't true, or buying things we don't need or want, perpetuating the cycle of crap.

Fake people

From the legions of flawless celebrities, to the friends who only post the edited highlights of their perfectly manicured lives (that's everyone then) the internet is a showground for fake people. But the birth of the 'influencer' has taken things to the next level. These shiny, happy people are defined by the Oxford English Dictionary as those 'with the ability to influence potential buyers of a product or service by promoting or recommending the items on social media'.

But hang on: why on earth (or online) should we be 'influenced' by people we have never met raving about things they have received for free? Despite the girl-or-boy-next-door persona, these self-appointed professional merchants of crap represent the epitome of faux-authenticity. It's a bizarre world where someone can be famous for being famous and can make a living from making deals with high profile brands simply because they have a lot of followers on social media (who may or may not be real).

The cult of the influencer is not without controversy: there have been cases of undisclosed affiliations and it turns out it's pretty easy to buy a mob of fake followers to make yourself look more popular – and therefore more influential. But aren't we missing the point? Influencers are by definition fake. They operate in a fake world, where their aim is to make us desire whatever clothing, cosmetics or holiday it's their 'job' to make us desire.

It doesn't really matter if they disclose their affiliations – that just tells you they are open about being biased, adding to the illusion of authenticity. An influencer who has been gifted an all-expenses-paid trip to a must-visit destination, is hardly going to point out the swarms of mosquitos, or the sanitary towels on the beach, or the queue of people lining up just out of shot for a turn on that legendary swing that sits in the ocean. They may have 325,983 followers, but that doesn't mean you need to join them. Cutting the crap online involves calling out this insidious form of crap for what it is: advertising – just in different (designer) clothing.

'Your time is limited, so don't waste it living someone else's life. Don't be trapped by dogma – which is living with the results of other people's thinking. Don't let the noise of others' opinions drown out your own inner voice. And most important, have the courage to follow your heart and intuition.'

STEVE JOBS

7 ways to help cut the crap online

We may not be able to curb the crap that breeds and multiplies all over the internet, but we can reduce our exposure to it and our response. Here are some easy ways to take back control.

1. Unfollow, unfollow, unfollow

The easiest way to cut online crap is simply to unfollow the people who are behind it. They could be influencers, uber-tweeters, nominal friends, serial boasters or anyone who spreads fallacies about global warming being a conspiracy theory, or vaccinations being a death threat. If in doubt, cut them out.

2. Declutter your inbox

If those 1,372 unread emails have been sitting in your inbox since 2017, there's a good chance you won't get round to reading them. They're just an annoying reminder of stuff you don't actually need to do. Hit 'select all' and exterminate them in one swoop. Then unsubscribe from all those irritating mailing lists with their needy demands for attention.

3. Slow down

The internet happens at car crash speed, meaning we have very little time to process or reflect on information.

In order to counter this effect, it's important to make time for activities that allow you to spend time in your own head such as going for a walk, doing some gardening or just taking a lunch break without your phone for company.

4. Make Screen-Free Sundays a Thing

Just as Meat-Free Mondays can help us cut down our meat intake, Screen-Free Sundays can help reduce the amount of crap we consume online. Having a whole day off – as opposed to just an hour here and there – provides a much more effective opportunity to engage with the real world and in real relationships. Of course, you could go further and make it the whole weekend.

5. Set limits

It's so easy to spend hours mindlessly thumbing through Facebook or Instagram. But every hour spent compulsively staring at a screen is an hour you will never get back. What's more, many of us are oblivious to the amount of time we waste online. Fortunately, there are a number of apps that will confront you with the truth, by letting you see your daily screen time and inviting you to set a limit. Do it!

6. Remove temptation

Our phones have become our personal assistants; we

rely on them to wake us up in the morning, to inform us of our next appointment, to tell us whose birthday it is, or to remind us that we've run out of bread. Yet if you find yourself inadvertently straying onto social media whenever you need to check the time or find out where you're supposed to be, consider getting a watch and a diary instead. The less you need to touch your phone, the less likely you are to abuse it.

7. Go on a social media diet

Our online lives can be dominated by the Fear Of Missing Out. But going offline – and especially off social media – enables us to discover the Joy Of Missing Out instead. You'll be amazed at how liberating it is to stop worrying about what everyone else is doing simply by not looking. If you don't feel ready to ditch social media completely, a less drastic option is to choose one or two platforms and delete the rest (obviously, don't just spend extra time on your chosen sites.) Alternatively, why not allow yourself one small browsing window a day? The less time you spend scrolling, the less crap you will be exposed to and this is one case where ignorance really is bliss.

> *'No price is too high to pay for the privilege of owning yourself.'*
>
> FRIEDRICH NIETZSCHE

Fake news

Did you hear the one about the new species of rat that can grow to the size of a watermelon? Don't worry, it's just fake news. Like fake people and fake followers, fake news flourishes in cyberspace. These are stories which appear to be true, but are in fact total crap.

But made-up news is nothing new. Urban myths have been around as long as fairy tales. However, when you consider that people under the age of 50 now get half of their news online, and people under the age of 30 get even more than that, it's easy to see how these fabricated stories can quickly become the equivalent of a box office hit. And while the substance may be fiction, the consequences can be real, influencing our decisions across every area of life – from the crap we buy, to the websites we visit, to the politicians we trust. And thanks to the omnipotence of the internet, it only takes a tiny percentage of people to be sucked in by a fake news story for it to have an effect, or even to sway a vote. Fortunately, fake news isn't all it's cracked up to be and you don't need to be a journalist to spot a dodgy story. A little lie-detection is all that's required.

5 tests to help spot a fake story

1. Be a cynic

Before gasping at a shocking headline, ask yourself: what is it trying to achieve? Does it want to convince you of a certain viewpoint? Is it trying to persuade you to buy something? Does it want you to click onto another website? If the answer to any of these is yes, then treat it with a healthy dose of cynicism.

2. Check and double-check the source

Have you heard of the author, or the publisher? If a story is published on a credible site like the BBC, Reuters, or CNN, then it's likely to be trustworthy. If on the other hand, it's published on a random blog, or website you have never heard of, it may not be, so check whether the story also appears on any other well-known sites. A word of caution though: even legitimate looking URLs can sometimes be fake, so double-check to see if it's been deliberately created to look like the real thing. Take a close look at the URL – anything that ends in '.infonet' and '.offer' rather than '.com' or '.co.uk' is likely to be dodgy. Or just check the real website's home page.

3. Read between the lines

A genuine news story will list the facts: it will give you the what, when, where and who of events. It should also include quotes from named experts and verifiable sources. If it doesn't, proceed with caution. A lack of facts and an abundance of opinion (unless it's an actual opinion article) is a sign that it may not be news at all. Other common giveaways include: a proliferation of spelling mistaekes (sic) poor punctuation and an overuse of exclamation marks!!!!

4. Don't believe everything you see

A picture used to be worth a thousand words, but in the age of digital editing, it may just support a lie. Common warning signs include: unusual shadows or an absence of shadows, jagged edges and strange perspective. If you think something looks amiss, it probably is. You can also do an online reverse image search to check whether an image has been modified or taken from another source and used in the wrong context to manipulate a story.

5. Go with your gut

If a story sounds too far-fetched to be true, it may well be fake. Although even stories that sound plausible can be made up, while some outlandish tales may actually be genuine. So employ a healthy dose of common sense and do a bit of digging as well.

> *'Beware of false knowledge; it is more dangerous than ignorance.'*
>
> GEORGE BERNARD SHAW

CHAPTER 3

CUTTING THE CRAP IN YOUR HOME

Do you long for a beautifully clean and organised house, but find yourself surrounded by crap? Are you forever tidying up, yet constantly losing things? Thanks to the ceaseless first world pressure to buy, buy, buy, most of us have an extraordinary amount of possessions, far more than we really need. Yet the ongoing accumulation of stuff doesn't make us happy; it can actually make us stressed, clogging our mental as well as our physical space. The good news is that when we make a conscious decision to live with less, we clear the crap from both our cupboards and our minds to make space for the things that really matter.

'Have nothing in your house that you do not know to be useful or believe to be beautiful.'

WILLIAM MORRIS

You may wonder what's the point of getting rid of the crap you've had for years. Perhaps you see yourself as a naturally messy person, or a bit of a hoarder. Perhaps you've just learnt to live with the chaos, in the same way as you might get used to living with a slightly smelly dog.

Many of us are so used to being surrounded by clutter that we barely even notice it. We have become accustomed to the pillar of magazines stacked in the corner, the stash of clothes lying in limbo between the laundry basket and the wardrobe, the heap of unopened mail on the kitchen table, the fruit bowl that's also home to a collection of pens, hairbands, batteries and Lego. These things have been around for so long that it's as if they no longer have a rightful place of their own. So what's the point of sorting them out? Does it really matter if the house is a bit untidy?

Unfortunately, when we get used to living with clutter and crap, we fail to see how much better, calmer and more efficient our lives could be without it. Of course, you could simply snowplough everything you don't use into the spare room, or rent a storage unit and shove it all in there. But getting rid of the junk in our lives isn't simply a case of 'out of sight, out of mind.' It's a mental process as well as a physical one. And this means adopting a new mindset and standing up to the more-is-better status quo.

Cutting the crap versus consumerism

Cutting the material crap in our lives goes against almost every cultural parameter. It goes against all the adverts, marketing tricks and promotions employed by those who want to sell us stuff. It goes against the murky part of human nature that covets what other people have. It goes against lust and longing and the idea that success can be measured in possessions. And most of all, it goes against the pervading belief that stuff makes us happy. It's surely no coincidence that the richest, most materialistic nations are also the ones with the highest rates of depression. Furthermore, it's in the interest of manufacturers to make sure that our desires are never fully met, which means we keep on consuming. This ensures we remain velcroed to the conveyor belt of upgrades, fast-fashion, changing trends and made-to-break products.

If there's one reason to cut the crap, it's that true joy doesn't come from material possessions. In fact, happiness comes from owning less, not more. If you're wondering how that can be possible, then here are just some of the ways in which living with less can enrich your life. No purchase necessary.

'An object in possession seldom retains the same charm that it had in pursuit.'

PLINY THE ELDER

13 good reasons to sort your crap

1. Your blood pressure could benefit

Have you ever spent a day blitzing your house, or even a single room, until there was not so much as a stray cup or hair in sight? Gleaming, junk-free worktops, floors you could actually see, a fruit bowl containing nothing but fruit. How did you feel? Like you'd just stepped into a spa? An orderly, yet homely environment doesn't just look more attractive, it feels better too, inspiring relaxation and tranquillity, whereas mess can make us stressed and anxious. Now imagine waking up to that clutter-free sense of peace every day – no toys to trip over, no piles of paperwork clamouring for your attention. And the best way to achieve this is to root out all the crap in the first place, so that everything that's left is a breeze to keep under control.

2. You'll be better off

Those hair straighteners you only used once, the box-fresh shoes you bought on a whim, the cross-training machine that's now a clothes horse. Selling off stuff you don't use can recoup some of your hard-earned cash. Try car boot sales, garage sales, eBay and the classified ads at the back of your local newspaper. Just make sure you don't use the proceeds to buy more crap! Buying less means more financial freedom to invest in the things that count: experiences, days out, time with family and causes you care about. Remember: the best things in life can't be bought on the High Street or the Internet.

3. It provides a chance to spread kindness

While higher value items can be worth selling, listing every last T-shirt and paperback on eBay is time-consuming and boring, so why not save yourself the hassle and give the bulk of your possessions away to charity or friends? Or sell unloved goods for a worthwhile cause. The knowledge that someone else may benefit from something we don't use can be worth far more than the cup of coffee it's possible to earn by flogging it. What's more, research shows that acts of kindness trigger the brain to release extra dopamine, the chemical that gives us a natural high.

4. It's better for your health

Having a house that's stuffed full of possessions provides an open invitation to dust mites and other nasties, and nobody wants to share their home with those, especially if they're likely to bring you out in hives. Just think about the bacterial colonies that could be brewing inside your granny's old armchair, or the germs lurking on all those unexplained spare toothbrushes loitering in the bathroom.

5. Cleaning will be less of a chore

While cleaning is a necessity, the less you have to do, the better. And the less crap you have around, the easier – and quicker – it is. An empty surface can take just seconds to wipe down, compared to one that's littered with dust-collecting ornaments. And that means more time to spend doing other things.

6. It teaches you to be decisive

Choosing which items to keep and which to discard forces you to become better at decision-making. This can then be employed in other areas of your life, too. And that can only be a good thing; nobody likes a ditherer.

7. It helps you to live in the moment

Hanging on to stuff from the past can keep us anchored to times gone by, rather than allowing us to truly relish the present. Of course, memories are important, but they shouldn't hold us back, either physically or emotionally. Whether it's cards and gifts from ex-partners, old CDs and memorabilia, or craft supplies you'll never get round to using, sometimes we need to have a clear out to move forward. So store the really special stuff in boxes and say goodbye to the rest, and let the 'good old days' occupy a space in your head, rather than your home. Similarly, don't be tempted to hoard stuff for the future:

the furniture you'll upcycle as soon as you have time, the dress you'll wear once you've lost weight or fashions change, the books you may one day read. The longer this stuff has been hanging around, the less likely we are to use it. Far better to let someone else enjoy it now, while you get on with the present.

8. You'll have more time

Does it take you ages to get ready in the morning because your wardrobe is groaning with so many clothes you can never find the ones you want? Have you ever been late for an appointment because your keys were buried beneath a pile of paperwork, or because you tripped over the jumble of shoes blocking the front door? When you live with less, you have less to keep organised. No sifting through piles of junk, or rifling through a forest of paperwork. And that leaves more time for better, or more important things.

9. It promotes gratitude

Carrying out a stocktake of all the possessions we've accumulated over the years can be a sobering experience, forcing us to confront our spending habits and own up to all those frivolous, regrettable and unnecessary purchases. Acknowledging the cost to ourselves and the environment, when so many people in the world have so little, can also be a valuable lesson in gratitude and accountability. It can make us think twice about making reckless purchases in the future and encourage us to cherish the things we care about.

10. It enables the best to shine

You wouldn't choose to hang around with people who don't make you happy, so why crowd your living space with objects that serve little purpose? When we cling to everything we've ever owned, we dim the value of the things we really love. Letting go of stuff that doesn't enrich our lives, helps us to treasure the things that matter most – whether aesthetically, emotionally or practically. So surround yourself with items that make you feel good and say goodbye to the rest.

11. It helps you to be more mindful

Mindfulness has become something of a buzzword, but essentially it just means paying attention to what we are doing in the present moment, and this is true for our shopping habits too. Often we purchase things impulsively, with little thought as to whether we will actually use them. Take all those items of clothing with the labels still attached, for example. What a waste. So going through our stash of clothes and other possessions can open our eyes to how much we own, and make us think twice about buying more.

12. It's liberating

Getting rid of the excess in our lives can bring an amazing feeling of lightness – both physically and emotionally. Saying no to material possessions, or giving them away, can help us realise we didn't actually need them in the first place. It shows that our belongings don't control us – we control them. With this comes an enormous sense of freedom; instead of striving for what's cool or current and trying to keep up with trends, we can just enjoy what we have. What's more, when we don't own something, we don't have to worry about losing it, or insuring it, or taking care of it, which gives us more opportunity to focus on people instead.

13. You'll be helping to save the planet

The profusion of material goods in our lives, homes and the world around us isn't just wasteful and extravagant, it's deadly. Land and oceans are being choked with waste and the weight of consumerism; natural resources are running out and the living world is dying. As we'll see in chapter 5, cutting the crap is about more than just decluttering, it's about preventing an unprecedented natural disaster.

How to start decluttering

If you've been living with crap for years, or have trouble recycling so much as a single magazine, the thought of decluttering can seem at best a little daunting; at worst overwhelming.

One approach is to start small and work up. You could choose to start either with a single room, or one category, such as clothing, cosmetics, jewellery or children's toys. You could even start with a contained area such as a desk or cupboard. Despite the insistence of certain decluttering methods, it doesn't matter how you go about getting rid of crap; the important thing is to make a conscious decision to start and then to get stuck in. Just find a way that works for you and fits in with your time and living arrangements. But if you need a bit of inspiration, the following technique can help get you going.

Step 1

Decide which area of your home, or category, you are going to tackle first. It could be your shoe collection, bathroom or the kitchen cabinet you don't dare open in case everything falls out. Hint: don't try anything too ambitious to start with.

Step 2

Gather everything from your chosen target into one large pile on the floor. That's right: take everything out, even the stuff you know you want to keep, leaving an empty room or cupboard.

Step 3

Put anything you definitely don't need or want in a separate pile. This could include things that you haven't touched in months, out-of-date cosmetics, or stuff you've simply forgotten about. (Don't worry, we'll come back to this rejection pile later.)

Step 4

Now return to your original pile and go through it again. Pick up each item, hold it closely and ask yourself whether you really love it, or whether it serves any purpose. If not, place it on the rejection pile. Try to be as ruthless and as objective as possible. (If you really have to, create a third 'don't know' pile.)

Step 5

Your original pile should now be considerably smaller than it was when you started. If not, repeat step 4! Once you've finished, return everything you want to keep back to its original place in in a neat and orderly fashion. This should be much easier now there's less to deal with.

Step 6

Return to your reject pile and organise the contents into five sub-piles: give away, sell, try to repair, recycle and throw away. Aim to throw away as little as possible. Don't be tempted to deal with these items later, put them by the front door or in the car now.

Step 7

Gather your 'don't know' pile (if you have one) into a box and store it away out of sight. If you suddenly miss something, or realise you can't live without it, you know where it is. After six months, repeat step 6 on any remaining items. If you don't have a 'don't know' pile, well done!

> ***'Organising is what you do before you do something, so that when you do it, it is not all mixed up.'***
>
> A. A. MILNE

Cutting the crap and the fashion industry

For many of us, the overriding source of crap and excess – not to mention expenditure – in our lives are the clothes that we wear. Or to be precise: don't wear. With finger-tap shopping and next-day delivery, the temptation to shop without dropping has never been greater.

No longer regarded as possessions to be carefully chosen and treasured, clothes have become as fast and fake as the fashion industry itself. How many items of clothing do you have lurking at the back of your wardrobe that you've worn just once or twice, or not at all? How many dresses with the label still attached, how many tops that don't quite fit, how many pairs of just-for-a-season jeans?

Research suggests that many of us use less than 50 per cent of the contents of our wardrobes. One survey found that in America, 82 per cent of clothes went untouched, with Canada and Switzerland close behind at 79 per cent, while the average Brit failed to wear 73 per cent of clothes in their wardrobes. That's billions of dollars' worth of unworn garments.

Besides the obvious hit on our personal finances, the cost to the environment is huge. For every 10 kilos of cotton produced, 10,000 litres of water are required. The manufacture of a single pair of jeans, for example, uses a staggering 35,000 litres. Then there are the chemicals

– more pesticides are used for cotton than for any other crop in the world, accounting for 16 per cent of global insecticide releases.

Synthetic fabrics such as polyester, nylon and acrylic also present a dire hazard to the environment. These fast-fashion fabrics are cheap to churn out, yet with every wash tiny microfibres no longer than 5mm are leached into the waterways, from where they make their way into the oceans, adding to the escalating problem of micro plastic pollution and the threat to marine life. Suddenly, those yoga leggings don't seem quite so in tune with the universe. Fashion changes, but that doesn't mean we have to follow it.

Stripping back your wardrobe

An effective way to weed out unused clothing is to pull things out one category at a time. So for example, start with shoes, then tops, then jeans and so on. Spread them all out in front of you, try them on if necessary, then choose which ones you want to keep. It's much easier to assess how many white shirts, black dresses, or pairs of jeans you actually need, when confronted with the whole lot in one go.

The touch test

Often, we hang on to clothes because we kid ourselves we

really do wear them, when in fact they get about as much exercise as the average statue. One way to demonstrate this is to turn around all the hangers in your wardrobe, so that the clothes are facing backwards. For folded items like t-shirts place them face down in the drawer. Every time you wear an item, return it to the drawer or hanger facing the right way. If after six months (or twelve months if you don't rotate your winter and summer clothes) some of the items are still looking at the back of the wardrobe, or the bottom of the drawer, that proves you haven't touched them, which means you probably never will, so let them go.

How to stop giving crap to children

As anyone with children, grandchildren, nieces, nephews, or friends with babies will know, little people attract a large amount of stuff. So large in fact, that people have whole toy rooms dedicated to containing the absurd amount of toys it's possible to accumulate in the first few years of life. But the thing is, when it comes to entertainment, children really don't need much more than their own sense of wonder and an innate desire to explore the world.

Of course, we all love to see a little face light up and hear the squeals of delight at receiving a new gift. But in reality most of it ends up joining the avalanche of broken, discarded and superfluous-to-requirement toys. Yet, give the average four-year-old an empty cardboard box and the chances are they will play with it for hours.

What's more, research suggests that too many toys are detrimental to development, hampering creativity, attention span and even social skills. On the other hand, children who are given fewer toys are less easily distracted and engage in longer, more inventive periods of play. Furthermore, they are more likely to value those toys and take greater care of them, compared to a child who has so many they can't decide what to play with. In the UK for example, surveys have shown that an average child owns around 240 toys, but plays with just 12 of them on a daily basis.

So while play is crucial to both childhood and development, it doesn't have to involve a glut of all-singing all-dancing toys. Resisting the urge to give in to the latest plastic-coated craze, or splash out on endless squishies, dolls and figurines, is liberating for parents, children, your home and the environment. And fortunately there are loads of crap-free alternatives. Here are just a few.

7 sources of crap-free fun

1. The linen cupboard

Although you can buy flimsy play tents, nothing beats making your own. Sheets and blankets draped over a table, clothes horse, or between two chairs, remains a timeless source of entertainment.

2. The great outdoors

As the saying goes, 'there's no such thing as bad weather, only bad clothes.' Sunny or splashy, children have a natural affinity for nature. It doesn't matter whether it's a park, a field, a back garden, or a whole forest, they just need the chance to explore.

3. The bath

No need for plastic ducks; sponges, cups and colanders will provide endless amusement, whether or not a wash is needed. On hot days, a large tub or paddling pool outdoors is even better. (Obviously don't leave young children unattended with water.)

4. A cardboard box

It may be a box to you, but to them it's a boat, a house, a fortress, a hideaway, and the perfect place for a snack.

5. The kitchen cupboard

As soon as they are mobile, most kids make a beeline for the kitchen cupboards, so you might as well give in. For children who are beyond the stage of putting everything into their mouths, pasta, rice and cereal make lovely sensory play materials. Pasta is also great for sticking onto paper or threading onto string. Wooden spoons, pots and pans make a great drum kit (if you can bear the noise). Alternatively, a mix of cornflour and water on a large tray should keep them quiet for a while and is strangely therapeutic for adults too.

6. An experience

For older children in particular, a special day out can have much more impact than anything that comes with a sticker saying 'made in China'. Try visiting a zoo, wildlife park or aquarium, going to a roller skating rink or trampoline park, a horse riding lesson, climbing experience, or seeing a show or the circus.

7. You

As corny as it may sound, your presence really is priceless compared to any present you can buy. So make time to chat, play, snuggle, bake or read together, visit the park, or just go for a walk or a bike ride. The enjoyment is likely to be mutual.

11 tips for keeping crap out of your life once and for all

Having made the decision to eliminate crap from your life, the second step is to keep it out for good. Here are some handy suggestions to help prevent crap from sneaking back in where it's not welcome.

1. Choose quality over quantity

It's far better to own a few things you really love, even if you pay a bit more for them, than a stash of stuff you bought primarily because it was cheap.

2. Avoid storage solutions

While stackable boxes, in-trays and magic clothes hangers might sound like a good way to organise your crap, in reality they just encourage you to cram more stuff into the same space, instead of getting rid of it. For most of us the problem isn't storage, it's hanging on to and buying stuff we don't need. The only solution to crap is to eliminate it.

3. Be a neat freak

Once a surface is clear, or a room is under control, a single pen or piece of mail can look out of place. Make a conscious effort to break old habits like dumping your keys, coat or socks wherever you happen to be and put everything in its rightful place as a matter of course.

4. Give your recycling bin pride of place

If your recycling bin isn't immediately accessible, then move it. If you have to traipse down the garden, or move things out of the way to reach it, it can be tempting to let stuff build up.

5. Become a borrower

The consumerist market dictates that we need to own everything we use. Yet this can be a ridiculous waste of money, space and resources. Libraries are a fantastic source of information and pleasure, but books aren't the only things it's possible to borrow. From toys to tools, there are rental services for all sorts of single use, short-lived, or seldom-required items from wedding dresses to wetsuits, bodyboards to lawnmowers.

6. Identify crap magnets

All houses have their problem zones: the kitchen table that's a dumping ground for kids' schoolwork and half-finished cups of tea, the fruit bowl that's home to loose change and hairbands, the bedroom chair that's permanently draped with half-dirty clothes and the desk with its jenga-sized pile of magazines and paperwork. Instead of letting things accumulate, tackle these areas on a daily basis to keep crap at bay. In addition, have a designated drawer or tray for things like hairclips and receipts, a noticeboard for letters and forms and fix a piece of string along a wall so that you can peg up children's artwork.

7. Say no to junk mail

Put a sign on you door saying 'no junk mail' or contact companies directly asking them to remove your name and address from their mailing lists. That's an awful lot less crap to deal with.

8. Play one in one out

Once you've discovered the joy of getting your crap under control, you need to keep it that way. One solution is to follow the 'one in one out' rule. So every time you buy a new piece of clothing for example, something needs to be recycled. The same goes for toys and gadgets. Similarly, resist the urge to buy new until you've finished with the old.

9. Don't drink and shop

We've all been there: scrolling away in the early hours of the morning, perhaps after a heavy night out. And before you know it, your bank balance has lost two decimal places and you're on first name terms with the courier. The best thing is to leave your phone alone at night. It's also a good idea to remove shopping apps and turn off one-click shopping – a recipe for debt if ever there was one.

10. Don't be a sucker for the sales

It's so easy to be drawn in by those big red signs declaring 'everything must go' or '50 per cent off'. In reality though, you probably won't be getting a good deal. Retailers commonly push up prices just before a sale to make the reductions look bigger than they actually are. What's more, a bargain is only a bargain if you actually need it, otherwise it's just superfluous.

11. Think of your relatives

If you don't sort your crap out yourself, at some point (in the hopefully distant) future, someone else will have to do it for you. So you might as well spare them the job (and potential upset, embarrassment and family friction) and do it while you can. There's no need to wait until old age.

'Happiness is a place between too little and too much.'

FINNISH PROVERB

CHAPTER 4

CUTTING THE CRAP IN YOUR FOOD

The irony of First World eating is that we can eat whatever we want, whenever we like, yet we are eating more crap than ever. More preservatives, more emulsifiers, more stabilisers, more refined products, more unpronounceable hidden ingredients, more chemicals. And these unsavoury extras don't exist only in junk food, they can be found in supposedly healthy products too. At the other end of the spectrum, healthy eating has become akin to a competitive sport, complete with rules, restrictions and (online) spectators. It's time to cut the crap – not just in the food we eat, but in the narrative that surrounds it – and to replace it with clear, straightforward sense and ingredients.

'Let food be thy medicine and medicine be thy food.'

HIPPOCRATES

We are living in the midst of a First World food war. On one side, streets are lined with fried chicken outlets and burger 'restaurants' and it's possible to drink an entire day's worth of calories in a single cream-laden, tooth-coating coffee. Yet on the other side, the list of prohibited foods becomes ever longer and the list of so-called 'superfoods' ever more bizarre (and expensive) thanks to an army of Instagrammers, bloggers, vloggers, self-appointed experts and celebrities. Camel milk, anyone? As obesity rates soar, so too does the neuroticism surrounding healthy eating.

According to the World Health Organisation, levels of obesity have tripled since 1975. Around the world, 39 per cent of adults are now said to be overweight, increasing the risk of numerous chronic conditions like coronary heart disease, type 2 diabetes and some types of cancer. As a consequence, we are bombarded with health education messages that implore us to eat less sugar, less salt, less fat, fewer carbs. There is little doubt that curbing the global appetite could save countless lives. But the real issue is not so much the fat or the sugar or the carbs or the salt, but the way they are manipulated into packet-to-mouth convenience foods that have become as normal as colour television. The easiest way to cut the crap from our diets is simply to eliminate, or drastically reduce, the amount of processed food that enters our mouths.

However, not all processed foods are equal, or equally bad. A processed food is simply a food which has had something done to it. It could be as simple as chopping or freezing, or it could involve a series of industrial processes and a whole menu of added ingredients – not just sugar, salt, fat and oil, but chemical flavourings, colours, sweeteners and emulsifiers – way beyond anything you would find in a normal recipe book. These types of foods are known as ultra-processed and can include things like pizza, fizzy drinks, pastries, confectionery, salad dressings, instant noodles and a plethora of other weirdly addictive or time-saving products that come under the general umbrella of convenience, but bear little resemblance to any real ingredients. Your body deserves better.

Unsurprisingly, studies show that eating ultra-processed food increases the risk of obesity, heart disease, high blood pressure, cancer and early death. But the high levels of sugar and sodium and the lack of fibre aren't the only things we have to worry about. Scientists have also speculated that the chemicals added to or produced during the manufacturing process may have harmful effects too. For example, compounds used in the packaging or storage of processed foods, such as BPA (bisphenol A) may interfere with the activity of hormones in the body, while other processes used to preserve meat may produce compounds called polycyclic aromatic hydrocarbons (PAHs), which have been linked to cancer. So if there's one form of crap we can all do without, it's the ultra-proccessed concoctions of cheap ingredients and chemicals that have the audacity to call themselves food. Here are just a few of the worst offenders.

6 things to cross off your shopping list

1. Processed meat

While unprocessed meat can provide valuable nutrients including iron, zinc and vitamin B12, other types of meat like sausages, bacon, hot dogs, ham and salami have been linked to cancer. The evidence is so strong that the World Health Organisation has ranked processed meat as a group one carcinogen – the same ranking as cigarettes, alcohol and asbestos. Findings show that 50g of processed meat a day – less than two slices of bacon – increases the chance of developing colorectal cancer by 18 per cent, due to the chemicals which are added during the processing stage.

2. Supermarket bread

For centuries bread was made with flour, water, salt and yeast. Then along came mass manufacturers who starting adding mysterious ingredients including calcium propionate (E282), emulsifiers like lecithin and enzymes like xylanase. And while these industrially added preservatives and processing aids might extend shelf life, prevent mould, or help the dough to rise, many have also been linked to health problems and allergies, including skin complaints and migraines. In the case of bread, the simple alternative is to make your own (it's far easier and less time-consuming than you might think) or to buy from a small trusted bakery or market stall.

3. Mayonnaise

For something that can be made from just three ingredients: egg yolk, vinegar and oil, it's astonishing to find that the average commercial mayonnaise contains up to 20 different substances including: modified maize starch, sugar, flavourings, guar gum, xanthan gum, calcium disodium EDTA and other equally unappetising sounding constituents. Yet what the manufacturers don't want you to know is that mayonnaise is surprisingly quick and easy to make at home by whizzing together those three basic ingredients – an egg yolk, vinegar and oil. The only extra you need to add is a little seasoning.

4. Vegetable oils

There is a common misconception that vegetable oils are healthy, thanks to a rather toxic combination of dubious research and some well-funded marketing. For decades, we were told to avoid animal fats like butter and lard in favour of polyunsaturated vegetable oils – the clear, tasteless oils like corn, soybean, rapeseed, safflower and sunflower. Yet recent research disagrees. These so-called 'vegetable' oils are actually made from seeds that were originally grown for industrial use. In order to make them fit for human consumption, they are refined, bleached and deodorised – a process known as RBD – using intense heat and toxic chemicals. The result is a product that is ultra-processed, and as it now turns out, has the potential to trigger numerous illnesses and inflammation. What's more, when it comes to animal fats, there is mounting evidence that dietary saturated fat is not associated with heart disease after all. So don't be fooled by labels like 'pure vegetable' and use olive oil or cold pressed (unrefined) rapeseed oil instead which are rich in monounsaturated fats; or saturated fats, like butter, coconut oil or ghee, which are more stable at high temperatures due to the higher 'smoke point'. And remember, it's not just the oils you cook with at home, many processed foods are also a significant source of industrial seed oils, so the more you can do without these, the better.

5. Margarine

The ugly sister of those odious vegetable oils, there is nothing healthy or natural about margarine either. There was a time when everyone ate butter. But then war was declared on saturated fats, resulting in a profusion of hideous, slimy yellow spreads. Closer in make-up to plastic than food, somehow this highly processed amalgamation of chemicals was considered an acceptable alternative to real butter. Fortunately, as the dangers of artificial ingredients, refined vegetable oils and trans fats have come to light, together with the research indicating that saturated fat may not be as bad as we thought, the tide is turning. Which is all the more reason to stick to real butter, ideally from grass-fed cows. Besides, the taste is incomparable.

6. Most breakfast cereals and cereal bars

While some breakfast cereals are so sweet they practically sparkle, others masquerade as the epitome of healthy eating. Yet many supposedly virtuous cereals like granola and bran-based cereals are also loaded with sugar. Look out for ingredients like dextrose, brown sugar syrup, sucrose, glucose, fructose, maltose, molasses, hydrolysed starch, invert sugar and corn syrup which are all forms of hidden or refined sugar. Your best bet is a bowl of unsweetened porridge or overnight oats. And while muesli bars are often designed to appeal to the health conscious, many contain just as much sugar as a bar of chocolate – and at least with chocolate you know what you're getting.

Cutting the crap on our plates – what's the alternative?

While there is a clear need to turn away from the crap that is processed food, that doesn't mean jumping from one extreme to the other, or swallowing the latest clean eating, paleo, keto, alkaline, or other craze of the day. Nor does it have to involve replacing junk food with obscure ingredients and exotic 'superfoods' and ridiculous dogmas, or eliminating whole food groups (unless you have a medical reason to do so).

Healthy eating isn't a regime, or a trend, it's about getting back to the foods our bodies need; food made in kitchens, not laboratories, the foods people ate before one in two of us got cancer and heart disease became the number one killer, and before anyone had heard of the word 'superfood'. In fact, the term 'superfood' on food and drink packaging was banned by the EU in 2007 (unless the product's health claims could be verified). Not that you'd know from a quick scroll through Instagram. The superfood hashtag continues to be ascribed to an ever-growing list of foods with seemingly magical properties, from blueberries and quinoa, to moringa, maqui berries, matcha and maca.

While such foods may contribute to a healthy diet, the propaganda that surrounds them only serves to create a kind of halo effect that makes certain foods look superior to others. Yet often similar levels of nutrients can be found in far cheaper, everyday foods that haven't been flown around the world and don't cost the earth. Blackberries, for example contain more than double the vitamin C of blueberries – and are freely available in season. Broccoli doesn't come with the price tag of kale, but contains many of the same vital nutrients including calcium, magnesium, iron, vitamin C and potassium. Sesame seeds contain many of the same nutrients (with higher amounts in some cases) as chia seeds, and lentils make a highly nutritious substitute for quinoa.

By focusing on a handful of costly hard-to-pronounce foods from exotic locations, we run the risk of overlooking the plethora of far cheaper, ordinary products that are full of nutrients without the hype – carrots, onions, cabbages, apples, eggs, beans and a multitude of seasonal fruit and veg. They may not be trending on Instagram, but they contain everything we need to live well, minus the crap that's found in processed foods and the crap that surrounds many so-called 'superfoods'.

Unfortunately, food, like everything else, is subject to the power of both marketing and fashion. Yet no one food will prevent cancer or heart disease, or meet all our nutritional needs; the important thing is to eat a wide and balanced diet full of natural, whole ingredients. Somewhere between food fanaticism and factory food, the key to cutting the crap is to refrain from ultra-processed foods as much as possible, and to treat the hype with a pinch of (pink Himalayan hand-harvested) salt.

What about veganism?

Talking of marketing and fashion, if there's one food and lifestyle trend that has eclipsed all others, it's veganism. Once the alternative way of life of a small number of ahead of their time hippies, veganism has gone from fringe movement, to hipster community, to dish du jour. It has shaken off its sandal-wearing, muesli-munching image to become about as mainstream as X Factor. Inevitably, multinational corporations have shown no hesitation in jumping on the bandwagon and cashing in on the trend. Regardless of their motives, it's never been easier to give up meat and dairy, thanks to an ever-expanding selection of vegan products in supermarkets and restaurants.

In addition, a wealth of evidence shows that veganism isn't just good for animals, but for the environment and humans too. Research highlights that a plant-based diet can reduce the risk of numerous health conditions, including: heart disease, Alzheimer's, various types of cancer, obesity, high blood pressure and type 2 diabetes. So far, so good. Yet on the downside, the soaring popularity of veganism has led to its increasing commercialisation, with the irony that many vegan products are as ultra-processed, or even more processed, than the foods they seek to replace. It's no longer just innocent veg and tofu on the menu, but synthetic burgers, faux nuggets, cereal bars stuck together with sugars and refined oils, and alternative milks and desserts swollen with starches, gums, and thickeners.

The problem isn't just the additives (although these are well worth avoiding) it's the fact that many of these products come in deliberately misleading packaging, designed to dupe consumers into thinking they are making a healthy choice. So while an informed vegan diet can be a healthy way of cutting the crap, it pays to read the label, or better still to cook from scratch using real ingredients.

What's more, while a universal switch to veganism is often heralded as an environmental panacea, the reality may not be so clear-cut. There is no question that we should eat more vegetables, pulses, nuts and seeds in order to reduce the rates of chronic disease. And there is no question that intensive, inhumane farming practices need to end. There is also no doubt that cutting back on meat consumption is a vital part of tackling climate change, since cows in particular emit huge amounts of methane which fuels global heating. In addition, they consume vast quantities of water, land and grain, adding to the ecological sabotage.

However, the demand for fashionable foods such as avocados and almonds also places a considerable strain on water systems, land use and transportation. Furthermore, extensive monocultures of industrially-grown crops such as rapeseed threaten biodiversity and pollute the earth with high levels of fertilisers, fungicides, pesticides and herbicides. On the other hand, free to roam farm animals can promote biodiversity and help maintain ecosystems, as well as help to improve soil health and fertility, actually increasing its capacity to store carbon. But until we can get over the hostility that exists between the vegan lobby and meat eaters, it remains almost impossible to discuss whether there may be a case for concessions on either side.

Ultimately though, whether or not you choose to eat meat, cutting the crap in food means eating locally, seasonally and sustainably. It includes cutting the chemicals that appear on the label, as well as those that don't. And it means being responsible for our own health, rather than recklessly colluding in the destruction of the planet.

Pesticides and other chemicals

If you've ever wondered whether it's worth paying extra for organic food, you'll be pleased to know that the nutritional quality of organic crops has been shown to be significantly higher than that of non-organic crops. An international team of experts led by Newcastle University in the UK, found that a number of key antioxidants – substances that can help protect against diseases like cancers, diabetes and cardiovascular disease – were up to 60 per cent higher in organically grown crops. This adds up to eating an extra one or two portions of fruit and vegetables a day, compared to non-organic crops. And it's not just fruit and veg. Organic meat and dairy products have also been found to be more nutritious, containing around 50 per cent more omega-3 fatty acids than non-organic products, as well as higher concentrations of some vitamins and minerals, such as iron, vitamin E, and CLA (conjugated linoleic acid) which has been linked to a decreased risk of cancer and other diseases.

But organic food doesn't just contain more of the good stuff, it contains less of the bad stuff, too. The research also showed that organic crops contained far lower concentrations of pollutants and potentially harmful chemicals. Cadmium, for example, a human carcinogen, was found to be almost 50 per cent lower in organic crops, while pesticide residues were four times more likely to be found in conventionally-grown crops. Of course, there is the argument that pesticide residues found on food (usually) fall within specified levels. However, it's hard to see how anything which is by definition lethal, can be deemed safe for human consumption – in any quantity. Furthermore, those residues persist even after washing and cooking. Few people would consider consuming a low dose of household bleach for example, so why should any other chemical be any different? What's more, some foods such as soft fruits, have been found to contain not just one but multiple pesticide residues and this cocktail effect may be of particular concern. Yet when responsibility is put before mass profit, it's entirely possible to grow food without the use of chemicals. The only type of crap that should be used for growing plants is natural crap – manure from chickens and free to roam farm animals – not industrial-strength lab-made potions.

Besides the clear benefits for human health, organically grown produce is also infinitely better for the planet. Intensive farming practices combined with the widespread use of pesticides and fertilisers are killing off insects around the world at an alarming rate. According to a global review, more than 40 per cent of insect species are declining and a third are endangered, posing a dire threat to pollination, food chains, ecosystems, food production and ultimately, the survival of the planet.

The scale of the problem calls for global and political action, but choosing organic is a vote for farmers who work in harmony with the environment, rather than against it. What's more, if half of all farming in the European Union converted to organic by 2030, it would reduce the amount of the EU's greenhouse gas emissions by almost a quarter, according to the Soil Association. In the UK alone, this would be like taking nearly 1 million cars off the road. So if you really want to cut the crap in your food – as well as the planet – choosing organic could be the best place to start.

9 more ways to help cut the crap in your diet

1. Plan ahead

We've all been there: you get home late, with zero energy and even less inspiration, so you end up grabbing a pizza or a takeaway, or eating a bowl of sugary cereal. Spending a few minutes at the weekend planning what you're going to eat for the rest of the week and putting in a food order, or doing a grocery shop, can help avoid falling into that midweek food coma.

2. Don't fall for 'fat-free'

If a food needs to persuade you it's healthy, there's a good chance it isn't. Fat makes food taste nice and removing it can make food so unpalatable it needs plumping up with other ingredients, like excess sugar or processed gums. You're better off just having the fat. Similarly, if a product is labelled 'sugar-free', check whether it contains artificial sweeteners. Healthy food speaks for itself. When was the last time you saw an apple or a carrot with a sign declaring its health credentials?

3. Cook once, eat twice

There's nothing wrong with eating the same thing two or even three nights in a row, or having leftovers for lunch. If you're cooking from scratch, it takes very little extra time and effort to simply cook a bit more. And that's one less meal you need to worry about.

4. Freeze it

Don't fancy eating your leftovers straight away? Then freeze them. Not just for ice-cream, the freezer is your best friend when it comes to avoiding food waste and almost anything can be frozen. It also means you've always got a meal in an emergency, or for when you can't be bothered to shop or cook.

5. Eat more plants

Whether or not you choose to go fully vegan, eating more veg is a great way to get more natural nutrients, minerals and fibre into your diet. It also means there will be less room on your plate for other crap.

6. Start slowly

If the thought of cutting out meat completely seems a step too far, ease yourself in gradually. Try committing to Meat-Free Mondays, for example. Over the course of a year those Mondays will all add up and the more you experiment with other foods, the more you'll build up a repertoire of meat-free meals that you might want to eat on other days too. Veganism can easily give the impression that there is no place for part-timers, but who says there are any rules? The impact on the planet – and human health – would be far greater if everyone gave up meat some of the time, compared to a small minority giving it up completely. In addition, setting yourself up for perfection can result in failure, causing you to give up. So start small and work up if you can.

7. Master a few basics

You don't have to become a restaurant-grade chef to eat good food, but learning how to cook a few simple dishes well is the cornerstone of healthy eating and means you won't need to rely on mass-produced crap. Soup, pasta dishes, lentils, basic risotto and meal-sized salads are all good places to start.

8. Grow your own

There's a general, but unfortunate, consensus that gardening requires a great deal of time and space and is an activity to take up once you retire. However, while only a few people can aspire to self-sufficiency, we can all grow at least a little of what we eat – a selection of herbs, some salad leaves, watercress or a few pots of strawberries. If you don't have a garden, all of these and many more can be grown in containers requiring little time or attention. All you need is a windowsill, a packet of seeds and some soil. What's more, gardening, even on a small scale, is a huge antidote to the stress of modern life. It takes us away from fast technology and fast food and helps re-establish the connection between real food and its source. And crucially, when you eat something you've grown yourself, you can be sure it hasn't been smothered in chemicals.

9. And finally: read the label

If you can't pronounce it or have never heard of it, it probably comes under the heading 'crap'. Avoid.

> ***'The food you eat can be either the safest and most powerful form of medicine or the slowest form of poison.'***
>
> ANN WIGMORE

CHAPTER 5

CUTTING THE CRAP IN THE ENVIRONMENT

(BEFORE IT'S TOO LATE)

The natural world as we know it is hurtling towards destruction. Carbon pollution from the burning of fossil fuels like coal, oil and natural gas, is heating the planet to crisis point. Our appetite for meat is eating away at the future. Rainforests are being mowed to the ground like grass, decimating countless plant and animal species, and pumping yet more heat into the atmosphere. Oceans are drowning in plastic, soils are awash with chemicals and insect colonies are disappearing by the day, threatening whole ecosystems and food chains. Clearly, this cataclysm of crap has to stop.

'The Holocene has ended. The Garden of Eden is no more. We have changed the world so much that scientists say we are in a new geological age: the Anthropocene, the age of humans.'

DAVID ATTENBOROUGH

It's an unfolding disaster, for which humans are to blame and for which we will ultimately pay the price, along with countless plant and animal species. Action needs to be urgent and radical, before it's too late. We need to cut the crap – the dirty fuels, the chemicals, the disposables, the rampant consumerism, the denial and the complacency. If we can do this, we have the chance to regenerate nature and restore the environment. The forecast is dire, but we still have the potential to avert catastrophe by changing the way we live. For the sake of future generations and our own, we don't really have a choice.

Addressing any problem involves accepting the underlying causes. To deny that human behaviour is behind global heating is like saying cigarettes aren't harmful. The link between fossil fuels and the rapidly escalating climate emergency is now unequivocal; carbon pollution has become an environmental cancer. And just as tobacco companies have been held to account for the link between cigarettes and lung cancer, it's time to stand up to companies and individuals who have an invested interest in coal or oil, or are supported by those that do, and who try to prevent clean energy for the sake of money or power.

Flaming fossil fuels

When we burn fossil fuels like coal, natural gas and oil, this significantly adds to the amount of carbon dioxide and other greenhouse gases in the lower atmosphere – along with other factors, like transportation and deforestation. Carbon pollution then causes the sun's energy to get trapped as heat: the more carbon is released, the more temperatures rise. This in turn causes ice to melt and seas to rise, leading to flooding and violent storms that destroy habitats, homes and lives, as well as other extreme weather conditions like droughts and heat waves, which are becoming increasingly common.

Temperatures around the world have already increased by nearly 1°C since the Industrial Revolution around 200 years ago, when machinery first began to take the place of manual labour. However, in the last 50 years, human activities have generated so much carbon dioxide and other greenhouse gases, that the additional heat has altered the global climate at an unprecedented rate, producing some of the hottest conditions on record. Each of the last three decades has been successively warmer than any preceding decade since 1850.

Scientists around the world have warned that if the current trajectory of global heating continues, the impact will be catastrophic, with irreversible consequences for both humanity and the natural world. Predictions include mass extinctions, super droughts, fearsome hurricanes and wildfires, crop failures and food shortages. Evidence suggests that essential ecosystems like coral reefs would be wiped out, and insects, which are vital for plants and crop pollination, would lose their habitats.

Adding to the misery, higher temperatures and altered weather patterns would have appalling consequences for hundreds of millions of people too, including reduced air quality, water contamination, poverty, a rise in heat-related deaths and infections carried by mosquitoes and ticks, as well as a huge impact on mental health. The World Health Organisation has described tackling climate change as a 'moral imperative'. The organisation estimates that between 2030 and 2050, climate change is likely to cause approximately 250,000 additional deaths per year, from malnutrition, malaria, diarrhoea and heat stress.

In order to prevent this dire scenario from happening, the rise in global temperature needs to be kept below 2°C, the target set by the Paris Agreement – an international treaty where governments pledged to limit the amount of greenhouse gases emitted by human activity. However, many scientists argue that the threshold of 2°C is still too high, and countries must do all they can to limit global temperatures to no more than 1.5°C above pre-industrial levels, in order to avoid the worst effects of climate chaos.

For this to happen, changes need to be implemented at a national and international level, including more investment in clean technology like wind and solar. While the UN has called for new taxes on fossil fuels and an end to subsidies along with stronger policies to bring down emissions and create a sustainable future, we can't just sit back and wait. We can't simply rely on governments to act, and to act fast. There are things we can all do on an individual level to help cut the crap that is currently destroying the planet. And although making personal changes can feel like a drop in the ocean, enough drops can make a waterfall, and a waterfall can lead to a river. We can't all crap in compost toilets, weave our own clothes, live in communal tepees and grow our own food. But we can all do something.

8 ways to reduce your carbon footprint

1. Skip the burgers

The meat and dairy industry is one of the leading contributors to climate change. Quite simply, every bite of a burger is choking the atmosphere, yet demand continues to grow. According to the United Nations' Food and Agriculture Organisation, animal agriculture accounts for 14.5 per cent of all global greenhouse gas emissions, while other experts believe the actual amount could be much higher. This is because animals, particularly intensively reared cows and sheep, emit vast amounts of harmful greenhouse gases. In addition, growing food to feed them requires enormous quantities of land and water. A global shift towards a plant-based diet could therefore be our best hope of avoiding catastrophic climate change. If you don't feel able to give up meat completely, start by giving Meat-Free Mondays a go, then aim to make meat a treat rather than a staple. So for example, instead of eating cheap burgers every week, have a free range steak now and then. Eating just one less burger a week can have the same environmental benefit as taking your car off the road for 320 miles and could reduce your carbon footprint by up to 50 per cent. If everyone did this, imagine the dent in climate change. In fact, a recent report in the journal Science described a vegan diet as 'the single biggest way to reduce your impact on planet Earth.'

2. If you need to drive, drive kindly

In a perfect world, we would walk, cycle, scoot and take public transport whenever we need to get somewhere. In the real world, cars are a necessity of modern life. However, you can lessen the impact on the environment by lift sharing and using leg power for short journeys. In addition, cut your speed to help save fuel and reduce emissions and switch off the engine when not moving, such as while stuck in traffic or waiting to collect somebody. Keeping your car serviced, with filters changed and tyres properly inflated, will also help it run as efficiently as possible.

3. Change your ride

Buying a car is hardly an impulse purchase, however, as soon as you are in a position to do so, consider swapping your petrol or diesel model for an electric or hybrid vehicle to slash toxic emissions.

4. Fly less

Swedish social media has a new hashtag. #jagstannarpåmarken translates as #stayontheground. Figures suggest that growing numbers of people in Sweden are following in the carbon neutral footsteps of climate activist schoolgirl, Greta Thunberg, and taking the train rather than the plane. There's even a word for flight shame – 'flygskam' refers to the feeling of being ashamed to take the plane due to the environmental impact. And no wonder: aviation emissions are a significant factor in climate change. One long haul return flight can add as much to your carbon footprint as an average year's worth of driving. The simplest answer is not to fly and to look for other ways of reaching your destination, or to take a holiday closer to home. If you do need to fly, you can help to reduce the impact by flying directly (planes use the greatest amount of fuel during take-off and landing) and by reducing the amount of luggage you bring, as the heavier the plane, the more fuel it uses. And while flying economy may not be the most comfortable option, it maximises the number of passengers that can be transported in one flight, making better environmental sense than flying first class or business class. And finally, choose an airline that seeks to reduce its emissions.

5. Use rechargeable batteries

Disposable batteries can release harmful metals such as mercury, lead and cadmium into the environment causing soil contamination and water pollution. Buying rechargeables avoids this and also helps to reduce the total number of batteries manufactured. And you'll never need to steal the batteries from the TV remote control again.

6. Reduce, recycle, reuse

Whether it's a frivolous plastic egg timer or a wall-sized TV, our consumption of goods feeds straight into our carbon footprint, driving energy-guzzling manufacture and transport. By choosing to buy less we can help make a tiny dent in the level of demand for new products, while recycling and reusing keeps items in circulation and out of landfill.

7. Change your loyalties

Refuse to support those who don't support the planet by voting with your wallet. If your bank invests in fossil fuels or turns a blind eye to the destruction of orang-utan habitats, move to one that doesn't. Likewise, switch to a green energy supplier that invests in renewable energy. And while supermarkets can be convenient, when possible try to buy locally grown products that haven't been flown around the world.

8. Make yourself heard

Write to government leaders and businesses, put pressure on them to invest more in sustainability, vote for leaders who put the environment at the top of the agenda, share articles that spell out the issues and inspire change, take to the streets to join demonstrations and call for action. Remember it's your world, as much as anyone else's.

More ways to cut the crap and reduce your energy bills

As well as helping save money, reducing electricity usage can also lower your carbon footprint by decreasing power plant emissions. It's not just about turning off the lights and other electrical appliances (although that's important too), it's about all those other small lifestyle changes. Here are some cost-cutting, energy-saving measures you can start today:

- Only boil as much water as you need – use a cup to pour water into the kettle, one per person.
- Wash clothes at low temperatures.
- Reduce the speed on the spin cycle.
- Turn off the oven and hob a few minutes early – food will continue to cook in the existing heat.
- Unplug your phone charger.
- Hang out clothes to dry instead of using a tumble drier.
- Turn down the heating – put on a jumper, take a hot water bottle to bed, or cuddle the person or pet next to you.
- Switch to energy-saving bulbs.
- Use a broom to sweep hard floors rather than a vacuum cleaner.
- Install a smart thermostat to help you track energy usage.
- When it's time to replace appliances, choose ones with the highest energy efficiency ratings.
- Invest in insulation and double-glazing.
- Make sure curtains and furniture don't cover radiators.
- Place a draft excluder under doors and stuff socks in the letterbox.

- Block off unused chimneys.
- Fill the dishwasher before letting it run.
- Install solar electricity panels. You probably can't do this one today, but you could save towards doing it in the future.

> ***'You cannot get through a single day without having an impact on the world around you. What you do makes a difference and you have to decide what kind of a difference you want to make.'***
>
> JANE GOODALL

Forests of destruction

On top of carbon emissions produced by industry and transportation, and greenhouses gases generated by animal agriculture, another major factor in climate change is deforestation. Rainforests are home to hundreds of thousands of species of plants, animals and insects, as well as communities of Indigenous Peoples. Yet according to Greenpeace, half of the world's forests have already disappeared, and only 20 per cent of those that remain are intact. They are being razed to the ground at a terrifying rate in order to provide grazing land for cattle, to make space for palm oil and soy plantations for animal feed, and to supply wood and paper products. In short, some of the world's richest resources are vanishing due to human greed and our insatiable appetite for crap.

Forests cover 31 per cent of our planet. Yet in 2017, the world lost more than one football pitch of forest every second. And in 2018, an area the size of Belgium was lost, according to data released by Global Forest Watch. The damage is so great, that scars left on the land can be seen from space. In addition to the irreversible effect on biodiversity, the threat to orang-utans and the loss of potentially life-saving medicines, the destruction poses a critical threat to tackling both climate change and the massive decline in wildlife.

Rainforests are crucial to maintaining the global climate balance and pumping oxygen into the world. Tropical rainforests are also the largest stores of carbon dioxide in the world. So when areas are destroyed, huge amounts of carbon dioxide are released into the atmosphere, trapping solar radiation and causing temperatures to soar even higher, further fuelling the climate crisis. In fact, if tropical deforestation were a country, it would rank third in global emissions behind China and the United States, according to the World Resources Institute.

Despite the grave forecast, it is still possible to turn the tide and preserve the remaining forests for future generations. In addition to the change that needs to happen at a global and governmental level, we can all fight back and make a difference.

> *'Never doubt that a small group of thoughtful, committed citizens can change the world; indeed, it is the only thing that ever has.'*
>
> MARGARET MEAD

Three ways to help save the trees (and the planet)

1. Read the label

Palm oil production is the largest cause of deforestation in Indonesia and other equatorial countries where orang-utan populations are plummeting as their habitats are demolished. Yet it's also the most widely consumed vegetable oil in the world and is found in around half of all the products we buy – everything from shampoos, soaps and cosmetics to pizza, ice-cream, chocolate, crisps and biscuits. And to make things complicated, it can also come under various other names including: Palm Kernel, Palm Fruit Oil, Palmate, Palmitate, Palmolein, Palmitic Acid, Palm Stearine, Palmitoyl Oxostearamide, Octyl Palmitate, Palmityl Alcohol and other equally obscure disguises. Yet according to the World Wide Fund for Nature, boycotting palm oil completely could make the situation even worse by encouraging companies to use other products that may have even more impact on the environment. Instead, look for products containing certified sustainable palm oil. Likewise, look for sustainable chocolate products – cocoa is another driver of deforestation.

2. Go paperless (or at least, recycled)

Cutting down the amount of paper you use is a simple step towards helping to reduce the amount of land deforested for logging. There are lots of ways to use less paper, including opting for bills, bank statements and other correspondence to be sent electronically rather than in the post, buying recycled toilet paper and other paper products and reusing gift wrapping or tearing out pages from old magazines to wrap presents. And don't forget to think before you print. (My very small contribution to this effort is that the paper used to make this book is from sustainable forests.)

3. Go retro

Instead of splashing out on new furniture made from poor quality wood, look for second-hand pieces, or those made from reclaimed timber. Besides the cool factor, making use of existing wood reduces the demand for logging.

> ***'A nation that destroys its soils destroys itself. Forests are the lungs of our land, purifying the air and giving fresh strength to our people.'***
>
> FRANKLIN D. ROOSEVELT

Craptastic plastic

In the space of one century, plastic has gone from exciting new invention to environmental nightmare. Cheap and ubiquitous, it has become the epitome of crap; symbolising both wanton consumerism and prodigious wastefulness. From the shoals of discarded bottles washed up on remote beaches, to the hideous mountains of eternal trash, to turtles choking on plastic bags, there is now no escaping this Frankenstein's monster of modern living.

The first completely synthetic plastic was Bakelite, made in 1907 by Leo Baekeland, who also came up with the word ‘plastics’ from the Greek plastikos, meaning ‘to shape or mould. Bakelite was derived not from plants or animals, but from fossil fuels. The invention heralded the start of a new era, leading to a proliferation of other now familiar plastics, including: polystyrene, polyester, polyvinylchloride (PVC), polythene and nylon. Since then plastic has infiltrated almost every area of our lives, offering a lightweight, affordable and long-lasting alternative to other materials.

The irony is that plastic is noted for its longevity, yet used for items that are often designed to be thrown away. It is this dual disposable yet non-disposable status that makes it such a present day evil. Because unlike organic material like wood or plants which are broken down by bacteria in the soil, petroleum-based products aren’t biodegradable. You can’t just throw them away and expect them to disappear.

The takeaway coffee cup, or plastic straw that is used for all of ten minutes, is destined to spend hundreds, or even thousands, of years in landfill. Multiply that by all the coffees consumed in just one day, or one year, and all the straws used in just one country and suddenly the problem is almost unfathomable. And of course it’s not just about cups and straws – plastic is everywhere, from food packaging to toys, car parts to computers, nappies to cosmetics, and even clothing. What's more, despite the common assumption that plastic is simply recycled, the reality is far less convenient.

> ***'We are at a unique stage in our history. Never before have we had such an awareness of what we are doing to the planet, and never before have we had the power to do something about that. Surely we all have a responsibility to care for our Blue Planet. The future of humanity and indeed, all life on earth, now depends on us.'***
>
> DAVID ATTENBOROUGH

Plastic: the not so fantastic facts

Only 9 per cent of plastic waste produced since the 1950s has been recycled, according to a global analysis. Of the rest, about 12 per cent has been incinerated, while the other 79 per cent remains in landfills or the natural environment.

- It takes about 450 years for a plastic bottle to break down in the ground.

- The equivalent of a truck full of plastic is emptied into the oceans every 60 seconds. That's eight million tons every year.
- It's estimated that by 2050 there will be more plastic in the ocean than fish.
- Many of the additives in plastics are toxic. Plastic buried in landfills can leach harmful chemicals into groundwater and the environment.
- Tiny plastic particles are swallowed by farm animals or fish, which are then eaten by humans. Minute plastic particles have also been found in most of the world's tap water.
- One million plastic drinking bottles are purchased around the world every minute.
- Up to five trillion single-use plastic bags are used every year.
- Approximately one third of plastic that is produced is used to make packaging.
- The production of plastic uses around 8 per cent of the world's oil production.
- More than 99 per cent of plastics are produced from chemicals derived from non-renewable resources such as oil, natural gas and coal. If the rate of production continues, the plastic industry could account for 20 per

cent of the world's total oil consumption by 2050.
- 50 per cent of the plastic we produce is used once and then thrown away.

9 plastic-busting alternatives

It would be naïve to pretend that by declining a straw or coffee stirrer, we can save the planet. But small steps do contribute to change, and the more people who get on board, the bigger the impact. What's more, refusing to be part of the plastic economy tells big businesses that they too need to change. Here are some things we can all try today.

1. Say no to single-use coffee cups and water bottles

Plastic coffee cups and plastic water bottles: just no. Get yourself a nice bamboo or stainless steel one instead and use it every time you go out. Refillables are the way to go and there's no shame in asking a café to part with some of their finest tap water when you run out.

2. Be a bag hoarder

Asking for a plastic grocery bag at the supermarket checkout is like breaking wind in a lift. Save yourself the social humiliation and carry spare bags at all times. Keep them stashed in your handbag, the car, your coat pockets, anywhere you can fit one in. For bonus points, keep some extras to offer to anyone who gets caught out at the till.

3. Don't fall for the testers

Yes it may be free, but that measly sample of yoghurt, or tiny splodge of hummus really isn't worth the plastic pot it comes in.

4. Make your own lunch

Apart from saving you the equivalent of a year's worth of gym membership, taking your own packed lunch to work (in a reusable container rather than a freezer bag) means you'll avoid all the packaging that comes with shop-bought sandwiches. When it comes to takeaways, bring your own fork so you don't need a plastic one. And while you're at it, why not take your own plate or container too.

5. Go large

Buy in bulk to reduce the amount of packaging. If possible, buy foods like cereal, pasta and rice from bulk bins or farmers' markets using your own container, if that's an option in your area.

6. Bring up a green baby

By the time they reach two and a half, an average child will have used approximately 6,500 nappies – that's a staggering amount of waste. Fortunately, re-useable nappies have come a long way since the 1970s and now provide a feasible alternative without the hassle of safety pins and soaking. What's more, as cloth nappies are free from the chemicals commonly found in disposables, they could be better for your baby as well the environment.

7. Have an eco period

All women should have access to sanitary items, however, most pads and tampons are laden with plastic. Fortunately, there are now an increasing number of more sustainable options including washable pads and re-useable menstrual cups. If you need to use tampons, then try using those without plastic applicators.

8. Be mean to your kids (and pets)

Young children can't always see beyond the shiny packaging, so it can be up to adults to step in. As well as resisting the urge to buy the latest plastic unicorn, light-up sword, or hideous dressing-up outfit, steer clear of food that comes with a side order of plastic too. It's time to put chocolate eggs and fast food meals which come with a side order of plastic on the naughty step – along with all the other mass-produced crap that will hold their attention for approximately three and a half minutes. And the same goes for animals: your cat doesn't need that squeaky neon rabbit and your dog will only rip that plastic ball to shreds. Let them play with a stick instead.

9. Look after your teeth

The next time you need to replace your disposable toothbrush, consider going for a bamboo version. You could use your old plastic one as a plant label, or for cleaning around the taps. You could even go the extra mile by buying toothpaste in jars (yes, it's 'A Thing') and making your own mouthwash using bicarbonate of soda and natural oils.

More crazily unnecessary examples of plastic

We have become so accustomed to the amount of plastic in our daily lives that we barely even notice it. Yet the vast majority of this plastic is completely unnecessary. Here are just a few products where plastic is simply uncalled for.

1. Liquid laundry detergent

Washing powder in a cardboard box does exactly the same job.

2. Ketchup and mayonnaise

Whoever thought squeezable condiments were a good idea? Apart from the waste of resources, you can never actually squeeze out the last drop. Buy a jar instead and scrape it out with a knife.

3. Honey

Bees don't need plastic and neither does honey. It tastes just as good out of glass. And see above for the issue of that last elusive spoonful.

4. Baby food

Pouches may be handy, but it's your little one's future that's at stake. Stick to jars, or better still, make your own when possible.

5. Pet food

Your cat really doesn't care if it comes in a squeezy sachet, or a tin. For dried food and treats, opt for cardboard boxes and leave the plastic alone.

6. Fruit and veg

Do apples grow in bags? Does nature shrink-wrap cauliflower? Do cucumbers need a second skin? If you can't get something unpackaged and can't do without it, then unwrap it at the checkout and let the shop know you would like to leave the plastic there.

'The Earth is what we all have in common.'

WENDELL BERRY

FINAL THOUGHTS

It's time to call time on crap. Yet cutting the crap is not a trend or a fad; it's about more than simply decluttering, or minimizing, or sorting out your wardrobe, or even giving up burgers and plastic straws. It involves overhauling our mindset in order to change our actions from the inside out.

This means making a conscious effort to challenge popular opinion and consumerist culture and to turn away from the modern frenzy of buying and having. It includes rejecting the way in which brands manipulate our insecurities, creating false needs and desires in order to turn us into 'consumers'. It's about recognising that we have a choice to step away from materialism.

Because when we stop believing in crap, we stop adding to the crap that already exists in the world. Only then can we become part of the solution rather than part of the problem. What's more, we discover that life can be so much more fulfilling when we stop wanting and embrace meaning and moderation instead.

Ultimately, cutting the crap is about cleaning up our act to help prevent planetary meltdown, mass extinction and human tragedy. It's about saving our children and future generations from an unimaginable and intolerable future. It's about making a world of difference, not just to our own lives, but to the world we live in.